EYE TO EYE WITH HORSES

Paint Horses

Lynn M. Stone

Rourke

Publishing LLC

Vero Beach, Florida 32964

www.rourkepublishing.com

PHOTO CREDITS: Title Page, pages 5, 8, 11, 14, 17, 18, 19 and 21 © Lynn M. Stone; photos on pages 6, 9, 12, 13, 16, 20 and 22 © American Paint Horse Association

Editor: Robert Stengard-Olliges

Cover and page design by Tara Raymo

Library of Congress Cataloging-in-Publication Data

Stone, Lynn M.
  Paint horses / Lynn Stone.
     p. cm. -- (Eye to eye with horses)
   ISBN 978-1-60044-582-8
 1. American paint horse--Juvenile literature. I. Title.
  SF293.A47S76 2008
  636.1'3--dc22
                                        2007019094

Printed in the USA

CG/CG

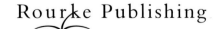

www.rourkepublishing.com – rourke@rourkepublishing.com
Post Office Box 3328, Vero Beach, FL 32964

Table of Contents

Paint Horses 4

The History of
    American Paint Horses 10

Being a Paint Horse 16

Owning a Paint Horse 20

Glossary 23

Index 24

Paint Horses

Imagine a dark horse of a single color, like black. Now, splash the horse's coat with white paint. The result? A beautifully colored horse that looks like it has been painted!

Fortunately, horses don't have to be splattered with paint from a can. Nature has done the painting.

Many of these horses are simply known as "Paints," or American Paint horses. Horses known as Pintos are also a mix of white spots and dark color.

A loud-colored Paint dashes through snow.

A registered Paint mare stands with her foal.

There is a difference between Pintos and Paints, however. To be **registered** as a Paint, a horse must have at least one registered Paint parent. Its other parent must be a registered Paint or a purebred Quarter Horse or Thoroughbred. The Paint, then, is what horse folks call a "genetic breed." A Paint's parents have to be of certain **breeding** and background.

PAINT HORSE FACTS

All Paint horses can be registered as Pintos, but not all Pintos can be Paints.

To be a Paint horse a horse must have one parent registered as a Quarter Horse, Thoroughbred or Paint.

On the other hand, a Pinto is known as a "color breed," like the palomino. A Pinto is a spotted horse, but it may be almost any mix of breeds.

This is a Pinto horse because it does not have a registered Paint parent.

Often stocky and compact, Paints can be good "cow ponies."

Paints, along with Appaloosas and Quarter Horses, are usually "stock type" horses. That means they tend to have a muscular, compact build. And especially in the past, Paints, Appaloosas, and Quarter Horses were widely used to herd livestock, such as cattle.

The History of American Paint Horses

Paint horses have been in North America for nearly 500 years. The Spanish explorers brought horses from Europe to North America.
Some of those horses were spotted.

Over time, many of the Spanish horses escaped or were released. The horses multiplied in wild herds. Among them, of course, were a growing number of spotted horses.

Spotted horses multiplied in the wild herds of the American west.

Plains Indians helped increase the number of horses with loud colors.

American Plains Indians captured wild horses and became excellent riders. At least some of the tribes, like the Comanches, especially liked horses in paint coats. By **selectively** breeding their horses for color, the Comanches helped increase the number of Paints.

White-spotted horses have always had plenty of fans and some **critics**. But the fans organized and founded the Pinto Horse Association in the late 1950's. Another group, led by Rebecca Lockhart in 1962, formed a Paint horse association. The new group wanted to **promote** unusual color patterns, too. But they also wanted registered paint horses to have stock type **conformation**.

Paint horse fans formed the American Paint Horse Association in 1962.

The dashing Paint has become one of America's most popular horses.

By insisting upon conformation as well as color, the modern American Paint Horse Association helps keep a reminder of the old American West alive and well worldwide. Today more than 800,000 paint horses are in the association registry.

Being a Paint Horse

Each Paint horse coat is a surprise! No two are alike. However, Paint horse coat patterns are grouped by color patterns known as tobiano, overo, and tovero, among others. A tobiano, for example, has white over its back. With the tobiano pattern, think of white splashed over the horse's back and down its legs. Paints often have blue eyes, but that is not a breed requirement.

A tobiano Paint mare stands with her foal.

A Paint casts a blue eye on the photographer.

A Paint's white hair can be in combination with any other **equine** color, such as chestnut, dun, gray, or black.

Interestingly, Paint horse parents do not always produce a Paint-colored foal. The youngster may be a solid color!

Paints are friendly and fun horses.

A big and muscular Paint.

Like their Quarter Horse cousins, paints have fairly short backs and heavy muscling on their hind quarters. A solid color Paint and a Quarter Horse would be difficult to tell apart.

Owning a Paint Horse

No one in the Old West wanted a working stock horse with a short temper. They raised horses that were calm, gentle, and willing. They also bred horses for intelligence and athletic ability. These are all qualities found in today's Paint horses.

This Paint is cutting – herding – a cow out of a herd.

Paints are a favorite pleasure-riding horse.

Many Paint horses are still working horses on ranches in North America and elsewhere. They are also raised for pleasure riding, trail riding, rodeo events, short distance racing, and the show ring.

A Paint weaves among stakes in pole bending competition.

Glossary

breeding (bree DING) – a history of an animal's parents

conformation (kuhn for MAY shuhn) – an animal's body shape and size

critic (KRIT ik) – one who considers something and often finds fault with it

equine (ee KWINE) – relating to horses

promote (pruh MOTE) – to give publicity and support to something

registered (REJ uh stured) – to have been listed officially in a breed book (register) as a member of that breed

selectively (si LEK tiv lee) – done after having made careful choices

Index

cattle   9

Comanches   12

conformation   13, 15

foal   18

Pintos   4, 7, 8

Spanish   10

spots   4

stock   9, 20

Further Reading

Denniston, David. *The American Paint Horse*. Capstone, 2005.
VanCleaf, Kristin. *American Paint Horses*. ABDO Publishing, 2006.

Website to Visit

www.apha.com
www.kyhorsepark.com/imh/bw/paint.html
www.ansi.okstate.edu/breeds/horses/paint/

About the Author

Lynn M. Stone is the author of more than 400 children's books. He is a talented natural history photographer as well. Lynn, a former teacher, travels worldwide to photograph wildlife in its natural habitat.